NOBODIES

IN A SOMEBODIES' WORLD

NOBODIES IN A SOMEBODIES' WORLD

MERLIN BYLSMA

the Write Place inc

PUBLISHING + DESIGN

ISBN: 978-1-7345829-7-0
Library of Congress Control Number: 2021920288

Published in the United States of America by
the Write Place, Inc.
For more information, please contact:

the Write Place, Inc.
809 W. 8th Street, Suite 2
Pella, Iowa 50219
www.thewriteplace.biz

Cover and interior design by Sarah Naberhaus,
the Write Place, Inc.
Cover stock image by Jennys_canvas, shutterstock.com.

View other Write Place titles at www.thewriteplace.biz.

DEDICATION

Dedicated to Holly, my wife of over forty years, and my children, Jennifer, Lisa, Bobby, Adam, and Amy. A special dedication to my ultimate somebody: my savior, Jesus Christ.

CONTENTS

INTRODUCTION

"Oh, I'm just a nobody."
"I'm not important."
"I don't really matter."

Have you ever thought or said something like this? I'll bet you have—maybe more than once a day. In a big world, it's easy to feel small and unimportant.

For many years, my wife and I ran elder care homes in Montana and Iowa. We cared for somewhere between three and four hundred people, and I can tell you that I've never met a person whose life doesn't matter. Even if someone's work isn't glamorous or goes overlooked, they fill a necessary niche. Of course we need doctors and lawyers and entrepreneurs—but where would we be without janitors, waitresses, power line workers, and the millions of others who make the world run?

That's why it has always greatly bothered me when people discount themselves as a nobody. All of us are essential.

Nobodies in a Somebodies' World is a series of essays on being a nobody. I hope these essays and the accompanying discussion questions encourage you to see yourself and others in a fresh light. I hope you will take pride in what you do, thereby becoming … a Proud Nobody!

CHAPTER 1

NOBODIES IN A SOMEBODIES' WORLD

Who is a "nobody"? If you ask someone on the street, they might say a nobody is a person who's not "important," who doesn't have power or authority, or who doesn't get a lot of attention. Well, that could describe a whole lot of us.

Let me introduce you to a few of these so-called nobodies.

First, I'd like you to meet Sam. Sam has had the same job for over fifteen years. He gets up at 4:30 a.m., drinks his coffee, eats some breakfast, and then heads to work. His job is one most people never think about.

Have you ever gone to a festival or a game and realized you have to use the bathroom? You look around and find a portable toilet—one of those plastic bathrooms they put up at all kinds of events. When you use one, do you ever stop and wonder who has to clean them? Well, this is where Sam comes in. He pumps everything out, power washes the units, and disinfects them. Most people never see Sam doing his job because he starts before they arrive. It's not the most glamorous job, but Sam takes pride in his work, and we are happy he does so when we need to use a portable toilet.

Next, let me introduce you to Lisa. Lisa is a single mom who has two kids and works at the local diner. She gets to work around 6:00 a.m., and she is there five days a week. As soon as she arrives, Lisa gets the coffee brewing and the silverware wrapped, then she makes sure the tables are clean and set up. Lisa's main job is busing tables after customers are done eating.

Have you ever stopped to look at your table after you have eaten and ask yourself, "Who has to clean this mess up?" Well, that's Lisa's job. She takes the plates and cups back to the dishwasher, dumps all the scraps and napkins, then wipes down the table and seats. Then she resets the table for the next group. Most of us never really see her because we leave before she even starts. Just imagine if Lisa did not do her job. How gross and filthy the diner would be!

Finally, I'd like you to meet Ben. Ben works from 11:00 p.m. until 7:00 a.m. at the local grocery store. He makes sure that all the shelves are fully stocked when customers come in each morning. He also makes sure all the shelves are clean and secure, so they don't fall down. Three times a week, Ben must also help unload the trucks that come in with a fresh supply of food and other goods. He divides everything up and puts it in the right place, so that it's easy to find each item when he and his co-workers need to stock shelves. Ben has worked at the store for eight years, starting when he was still in high school. Like Sam and Lisa, we don't often see Ben. The store is closed when he is at work.

So many nobodies doing important work we don't notice. Think of the people who keep the power on in your home. What happens when a winter storm comes through and knocks the power out? Who has to go out in that bad weather to fix the power lines so you can be safe and warm? Or what about those nobodies who clean up in the hospital after a surgery? Sometimes that is a very gross and bloody job. It's also one hardly anyone sees or thinks about.

Taking notice is the first step in understanding the importance of nobodies. Try looking for them today—you may be surprised by how many you find!

Discussion Questions

Think of a time you called yourself a "nobody." What did you mean?

This essay describes several important jobs that happen behind the scenes. Can you think of any other examples? Who typically does these jobs?

Have you ever been in a position where no one noticed you, or they didn't recognize the importance of your work? How did that make you feel?

CHAPTER 2

A DAY IN THE LIFE OF A SOMEBODY

I want you to meet John—a man most would call "a somebody." He is the founder and CEO of a company that employs over ten thousand people. He has run this company for twenty years and made it very profitable.

Let's take a look at a typical day in John's life.

John has been married to his wife for twenty-five years, and they have two children. They live in a very prestigious neighborhood and enjoy all the finest things money can buy.

John's day starts at 6:00 a.m., when he rises and showers. He has breakfast with his wife before being picked up by his driver. As he goes to work,

John looks out over his well-manicured estate, with its vast lawn and the stream that runs through it. His car passes through the gate and begins the twenty-five-minute drive to his office.

When John is dropped off at the front of his building, he is welcomed and goes up to his lush office on the tenth floor. When he arrives, he is greeted by his personal secretary, who has worked for him for over fifteen years. His coffee is already on his desk, complete with two shots of cream and two scoops of sugar. John and his secretary go over his very full schedule of phone calls and meetings. She fills him in on the business trip scheduled for next week. John will be gone for three days.

At 11:30 a.m., John meets with the company's vice president, who catches him up on the latest developments. Lunch is all set up for them, with meals and drinks ordered and ready at the appropriate time. This meeting lasts for three or four hours, and John is given all the files and proposals he needs to review.

At 4:00 p.m., John goes to work out in the gym on the first floor of his office building. His personal trainer meets with him regularly and takes him through a custom exercise program. After a quick shower, John meets his wife at a dinner with some close friends. Afterward, they take in a show and end up at home around 10:00 p.m. The lights are on, their bed is turned down, and some ice water is on John's bedstand, along with the book he has been reading.

Life is very good. John is blessed each day.

Now let's take a look at how many nobodies it takes for John to enjoy this life.

First, we must meet Meg, who comes to the house at 6:00 a.m. six days a week to cook breakfast for John and his wife. She makes all the meals for the family and has done so for eighteen years.

Next there is Joe, who has been the chauffeur for the family for sixteen years. He also takes care of the cars, making sure they are filled with gas and serviced as needed. Joe takes each family member to their appointments at the proper time.

José and Seth take care of the lawn and gardens on John's property. They mow, trim, weed, and prune. They are also responsible for snow and ice removal in the winter.

When John gets to his office, his personal secretary, Steph, sees to it that his schedule is kept and his meetings are on time. She makes sure coffee is ready by the time John arrives each morning. Steph screens all of John's calls to make sure he is not bothered by unwanted interruptions. She reminds him of his meetings, and she takes notes during all of them to keep track of what was discussed and decided. Steph travels on business trips with John and makes all the needed arrangements.

In addition to Steph, John has two other secretaries who take care of all the paperwork, letters, and other mail. They also file and take some of the phone calls that come in.

The finance department takes care of payroll and bookkeeping. Yet another department handles all hiring and firing. In the lunchroom, over ten people prepare food, serve meals, and clean up.

John's personal trainer is named Shane. He helps John stay fit and healthy.

When John gets back home, his house is always clean, with the beds made, bathrooms shining, floors vacuumed and mopped, windows spotless, and laundry folded and put away. This is all thanks to Shawna and Teresa, who have been with John's family for fourteen years and take care of all the housekeeping.

In short, it takes a lot of nobodies to make John's life so enjoyable. That is the case for all the somebodies in our world: the CEOs, actors, multi-millionaires, and politicians … even the president of the United States. These somebodies can enjoy their lives because the nobodies perform all these tasks for them.

Ask yourself: Who cooks the meals at the White House? Who cleans the bathrooms? Who does the laundry?

These people may be thought of as nobodies, but they are absolutely critical to the lives of the somebodies. They deserve both thanks and gratitude.

Discussion Questions

Who are the nobodies who make your life possible?

Are you the essential nobody in someone else's life?

Do you think nobodies are always treated fairly? Why or why not?

How can you show gratitude to the so-called nobodies of our world?

CHAPTER 3

THE ESSENTIAL NOBODIES

In 2020, we heard a lot about essential workers. But what does this term mean? Aren't we all really essential? Are there any essential workers we could do without?

In the previous chapters, I've asked you to notice and thank the people who cross your life whom you may not have thought about before. Now I ask you to dive deeper. If you can, find out the name of the garbage man who picks up your trash, or the people who work at the grocery store where you buy your food.

Have you ever really talked to the people who work at the gas station? Or the workers who keep your town or city running smoothly? How about the crews who fix your roads or remove snow and ice? Most of the time, they've finished before you even wake up.

So many essential people impact our lives. If they did not do what they do each and every day, our lives would be completely different and, in some cases, very inhospitable.

We are *all* essential in this world. Ask yourself whose life would be affected if *you* did not do what *you* do. You might not have a big impact on the somebodies we discussed in the previous chapter, but you are truly needed by the people who surround you.

Last Sunday, when I was in church, I looked around at all the people in the pews. Most of them did not have an active part in the service, but if they weren't there the praise team would be singing to an empty building. The pastor would be preaching to a vacant room. These people might be what they call "pew warmers," but they are what makes a church a community.

I've asked you to become aware of those around you who make our world work and give them a thank-you. While you're at it, take noticed of how much *you* make a difference. You are essential. You matter and can become a very Proud Nobody!

DISCUSSION QUESTIONS

When you hear the term "essential worker," who do you think of?

Is there any work that is *not* essential?

DISCUSSION QUESTIONS (CONTINUED)

How are you essential to the people in your life? To your community?

CHAPTER 4

PROUD PARENTS OF A NOBODY

When I drive in traffic, I often see bumper stickers that read: "Proud Parent of an Honor Student" or "Proud Parent of a Marine." But have you ever seen one that reads, "Proud Parent of a Nobody"?

Today, we push our kids to become the somebodies. Sports figures, actors, doctors, lawyers, and many other things. These are all good goals, but how many times do we tell our kids to become great factory workers, bakers, custodians, servers, etc.?

My wife and I have five kids, and none of them are in what's considered the top vocations. They are a factory worker, a nursing home worker, an assistant administrator at a church, an assistant administrator at a resort, and a finish carpenter. All of them show up for work each day, do their jobs well, and go home to their families at night. Are we proud parents? For sure! We are so proud of who they are and what they have become.

Few kids grow up and climb to the top pinnacle of the workforce. That means many become the nobodies you've been reading about who are so important to our lives. And many of these nobodies have parents who are proud of them for what they do.

We need to make our kids aware of how important they are to every one of us, no matter their profession. We need to remind them of who benefits from the work they do.

Just imagine how well our kids would mature if they understood the importance of who they are and what they become. I have seen many top athletes, actors, and even doctors and lawyers who have reached the top of their fields only to realize they still do not feel fulfilled or complete.

Some people have earned a Ph.D. and made more money than they could spend, only to find happiness being a counselor or owning a restaurant or kids' camp. They have found their true calling and fulfillment in what they do now.

Would they have been better served if they'd been told their current career would be so important and bring them so much happiness? Or that their parents would be just as proud of them, no matter what they chose to do?

Now, I'm not saying you shouldn't follow your calling if it is to be an actor or a lawyer or a doctor. If that is what you want to do, then make sure you put in the effort and become what you were meant to be. Just make sure the path you follow is what fulfills *you* and makes *you* happy each day.

DISCUSSION QUESTIONS

Are you happy and fulfilled in your work? Why or why not?

Were you pressured to follow a certain career or educational path? If so, how did you deal with that pressure?

If you could turn back the clock, would you make the same choices in your career? Or would you make different choices?

What advice would you give to a high school or college student considering their future job?

CHAPTER 5

FIELDS OF NOBODIES

The other day, I took a walk to the cemetery to visit my parents' gravesite. While I was there, I looked out over the many, many headstones. I thought to myself, *Who were all these people?* I started walking around the headstones and saw the names of people who had been the *somebodies* of our town when I was young. One had been the mayor for many years. Another had been a big businessman. Still another had been a big-time farmer in our area. I even saw the headstone of a founding member of the group who established the town.

I read the dates on the headstones. Some were buried fifty years ago. Others seventy years ago. Still another was laid to rest two hundred years ago. Again, I thought to myself, *Who really were these people?* They didn't appear to have been visited by anyone. There were no flowers or ornaments on their graves. Back in town, I asked around to see if anyone had known or known of them. Some had never heard of these people, while others remembered them but didn't really know much about them. Most of their family members had moved away.

As I looked over this sea of headstones, I was amazed to think of it as a field of nobodies. Most people had forgotten who these people had been and what they had done and accomplished.

We must realize that we will all become part of this sea of nobodies at some point. In fifty or seventy years, who will remember who you were or what you did? Yes, your family members will recall those things about you, but memories fade. Just think back twenty or thirty years ago and try to recall what your family members were doing.

We learn about presidents, members of Congress, and big businessmen, but we don't know them personally or remember everything they did. Outside school, we think back to the person who installed the first furnace in our homes or our air conditioners. And the person who sold us our first computer or TV. We remember some details, but all of these gadgets keep advancing so rapidly. We don't recall how they were years ago, let alone who sold them to us.

We all work to accomplish things and make a difference in the world. But in the end, what will we really be remembered for? I think we remember people who have made an impact on who we are as a person. That teacher who took an interest in you and believed in you. Or that spiritual advisor who cared enough to talk to you and answer your questions. These are the people we remember and care deeply about.

DISCUSSION QUESTIONS

In this essay, a cemetery is described as a "field of nobodies." What do you think of that description?

Have you ever wandered around a cemetery and looked at the headstones? What did you think about as you read the names and dates of the people buried there?

Do you tend to remember more about a person's accomplishments or about the way they made you feel?

CHAPTER 6

HOW A NOBODY CAN BECOME A SOMEBODY

What is the one thing nobodies have in common? You really don't know who they are! Picture someone you would think of as a nobody. Do you know anything about them? How many people are in their family? How long have they been married, or are they divorced? What do they do for work? How long have they been at their job? How many kids do they have, and how old are they?

Once you get to know someone, you no longer look at them as a nobody. You start thinking of them as a real person, as someone you care about.

I once had a co-worker who was not very friendly. He never really talked or smiled. He always seems to be in a bad mood. I didn't make any effort to get to know him or even talk to him until I heard one of my other co-workers talking about him. Come to find out he was divorced, and his ex would not let him see or even call his kids. He had tried to self-medicate with drinking and drugs, which got him in trouble with the law. All of this caused him to be evicted from his apartment, so he had been sleeping in his car. Life kept getting worse and worse for him.

Once I started to learn about him, I could feel for this co-worker and imagine what life must be like for him. I tried harder to smile at him, talk with him, and help or listen to him. A lot of the time he just needed someone to listen to him vent without judgment. I got to know him, and as a result I began to think of him as a somebody.

If we pay more attention to people and discover their stories, we begin to look at them differently. We become invested in their lives and want to make a difference for them. Then they start looking at us differently too—they see us as a caring person.

Discussion Questions

Is there someone in your life you would like to know better? How could you go about building a relationship with them?

Think of a time when someone made an effort to get to know you. Maybe it was at work, at church, at school, or somewhere else. How did it make you feel?

Have you ever had an incorrect first impression of someone? How did your perception of them change as you got to know them?

CHAPTER 7

THE NOBODY WHO BECAME THE GREATEST SOMEBODY

He was born in a small town named Bethlehem. When His mother went into labor, His parents were not able to get a proper room. After He was born, He was placed in a manger (or feeding trough). Soon after, He had to flee with His mom and dad to Egypt because somebody wanted to kill Him.

He was given the name Jesus. His dad was a simple carpenter, His mother a teenager. They were a humble couple—not the high-class parents you would expect for Him.

After living in Egypt for a while, the family made their home in Nazareth, another nothing town. (Remember John 1:46: "Nazareth! Can anything good come from there?") Nazareth was set in a small basin surrounded by hills, and it wasn't very accessible. It did have a water supply called Mary's Well, and there was limited terraced agriculture and pastures for grazing. But other than that, there wasn't much to it.

Jesus spent most of His childhood in Nazareth, and we are not told much about His time there. The Bible does mention that He went with His parents to Jerusalem when He was twelve, where He amazed many older priests.

At thirty years of age, Jesus began His ministry and was baptized by John. Afterward, He was led into the desert and withstood forty grueling days and nights in the wilderness. Soon after, Jesus performed His first miracle: turning water into wine at a wedding. This moment was significant, because it pointed to who Jesus really was and why He had come.

The Bible tells us that at the wedding, Jesus asked the servants to take six large stone vessels (six is the number for man) and fill them with water (which stands for cleansing). He blessed the vessels, and the water turned into wine (which represents the blood shed for our sins). We see echoes of this story at Jesus' crucifixion, when soldiers pierced His side and water and blood came out. Man was cleansed by the washing away of his sins by the blood shed by Jesus.

So who really was Jesus, a man who started His life as a nobody? The Bible tells us He was with the Father from the beginning of the world, then emptied Himself and became nothing (Philippians 2:5–8). He became a servant. He became human and lived a selfless, obedient life, then died a selfless, obedient death. By doing all this, Jesus became the greatest somebody the world has ever known. All who believe in Him are given eternal life. He will be the King of Kings and Lord of Lords!

We all must contemplate how someone so great and awesome became a nobody, so each of us could become an eternal somebody who will reign with Him.

Discussion Questions

The Bible doesn't share much about Jesus' childhood. How do you picture His early years? Do you see any similarities with the life of a modern nobody?

In Jesus' day, Nazareth was dismissed by some as a nothing town. Are there any places like that today? Have you ever lived in one?

Why is it significant that Jesus lived the life of a nobody until His ministry began?

Listen to the song "Nobody" by Casting Crowns. How do the lyrics relate to the theme of this essay and this book?

CHAPTER 8

HOW WE JUDGE NOBODIES

I've observed people over many years, and I'm always amazed by how we rank other people and ourselves. We decide if a person is a somebody or a nobody, and that judgment dictates how we treat them.

If you meet someone with a fancy car, stylish clothes, or a large house, how do you treat that person? Now, let's say you meet a homeless person, whose appearance is dirty and messy. How do you treat them? Picture a person with many college degrees and someone who barely has their high school diploma. How do you look at each of them?

During her career, my wife took care of many of the residents in our elder care homes. Residents often would not make it to the bathroom on time and would have an accident. She would help them get cleaned up and changed.

I asked her once, "How do you do that? Many people couldn't do that, even for their own family." She just smiled and said, "Somebody has to help. If my mom and dad needed help like this, I hope somebody would help them. Just think if nobody helped these people. What kind of a mess would they have? What sores would they have? How degrading would it be to who they are as a fellow human being?"

She did her work without judgment, which is so important. The difference she made in these lives made her a somebody to these people and their families.

So many people are judged or looked down on for doing humble jobs. Nobody notices them, but if they didn't do their work our world would be more difficult and unpleasant to live in. Think of your garbage man, a hog farmer, or someone who works on the sewer lines. The next time you go to the airport, ask yourself how many nobodies make your trip possible. Think of the luggage handlers, the janitors who keep things clean, the people who check the plane to make sure it's safe, those who deice the plane, the ticket clerks, the people in the control tower who determine when it's safe to land or take off. All these people are needed to make sure you have a great, safe flight.

Now ask yourself: Do you even notice these people? You definitely would if there was a problem ... but what about when things run smoothly? Do you judge them negatively or positively for the work they do?

When you make an effort to see everyone for what they are—essential and important—you don't judge others as nobodies. They are a somebody to you, even if you don't know them personally.

Discussion Questions

Have you ever been judged based on your profession, wealth, education, or appearance? What was that experience like?

Do you find yourself, consciously or unconsciously, judging others based on what they do or how they look?

How can we recognize and challenge the snap judgments we make about other people?

CHAPTER 9

BECOMING A PROUD NOBODY

The world is made up of billions of people. Each person fills a necessary niche for the good of all. Have you ever stopped and asked yourself or those around you: "Why do you do what you do?"

I have asked people this question and heard many answers. Many tell me they don't know why they do what they do. Others say it's for the money. Still others say they've never really thought about it. I've asked myself this question and found I didn't know the answer. Was it just for the money, or was it the only work I could find? Was it what I was made to do, or was it what God made me to do? I took all this into consideration and came up with this answer: I did the work I did because there were more things I liked about it than things I didn't like about it.

We decide what path we follow. No one forces us in a particular direction. (Perhaps that's the case in other countries, but not here.) There are very few somebody positions compared to the millions and millions of so-called nobody positions that are essential to everyday life. What would our world be like if we had no one to pick up garbage, bake bread, clean buildings, or care for older people who have had an accident? Think of all those positions we take for granted. We see somebodies on TV and think of them with high esteem … but who are the people behind the cameras? Who runs the light or the sound? Who does hair and makeup? We never see them, but they are essential.

Now think about what you do: Who do you affect?

Know that you are needed in your town, your job, your home, and your family. Take pride in what you do and understand it is truly important for the good of us all. If you really don't see any worth in what you do, make a change. Find something that makes you feel like you are filling a need. Be a Proud Nobody, because really there are no nobodies—just underappreciated essential workers!

I would like to thank you for doing what you do. Whatever it is, it really is important and necessary.

DISCUSSION QUESTIONS

Why do you do what you do?

How would the world be affected if you *didn't* do your job?

Discussion Questions (continued)

Do you agree there are no nobodies, just under-appreciated essential workers?

Do you think of yourself as a Proud Nobody? Why or why not?

CHAPTER 10

THE NOBODY HEROES

As a kid, my heroes wore capes and tights, or they donned white cowboy hats and rode horses. Now that I'm older, I find that my heroes are nobodies. Let me explain.

Some of my heroes live in other countries, and they run a group that buys slaves. Yes, they buy slaves—men, women, and children purchased for fifty dollars each. Can you believe that in these days you can still buy slaves?

Now let me explain what this group does after they buy these people. They feed them, give them medical care, and bring them to a safe place. They nurse any wounds or medical conditions until the person is healthy. Once they are in good health, the group helps them find a safe place to live, as well as a job or a way to support themselves. They also try to help them find any family they have (which is sometimes impossible because their families are the ones who sold them to the slave traders). All of this is done safely and securely using the internet. Hundreds of people have been set free and their lives saved by this group—all in the name of Jesus and with His love.

Another hero of mine is a lady who was very successful in her life. She went to a county where she found children being trafficked to sex slave groups. She was so angered at seeing children as young as two and three being abused that she started a group that rescued these kids. She started orphanages to house and care for these children and keep them safe. She also started schools to teach these kids how to read and write.

This mission is very dangerous because the people running these operations are not happy about it. She has been captured, beaten, and raped by them. But she keeps going and will not stop. Her story is an inspiring example of what can be done for the least of these. She continues to rescue kids and build schools and orphanages, and she has made it possible for many kids to graduate and find a real and beautiful life.

I have one final example of my nobody heroes. This group was set up in Guatemala, which is being decimated by HIV/AIDS. Whole families have been wiped out, and lots of little children have been left alone. This group has started orphanages to care for these children, feeding, nursing, and loving them as their own. These caring people have often held little children and babies in their arms as they died, unable to do anything for them except humbly and tenderly show them they are loved and are important. When the children leave their arms, they go into the arms of their Heavenly Father.

These are the people I look to as my heroes. In some cases, I don't even know their names, or I can't because it would put them in danger. Someday, these heroes will be welcomed home with cheers from their Heavenly Father for a job well done.

DISCUSSION QUESTIONS

Who did you look up to as a hero when you were a child? Who do you consider a hero today?

Can you think of any examples of a nobody hero?

Have you ever been inspired by your heroes to take action?

Is there a cause you care about that you'd like to get involved in?

POEM

A PROUD NOBODY

I may not have the sweetest voice
to thrill the crowd with song.
I may not have an authoritative voice
to make them hang on every word.
I may not have the wealth in hand
to give to the needy throng.
But I do have a blessed life,
and I mean the world to family dear.
I've held a child, a grandchild,
and loved ones in arms so tight.
I've been the name that someone called
when pain or sorrow was in their heart.

I can keep my town and county clean,
make it a safe and scenic place to live.
Yes, you may never hear my name on untold lips,
but I will take my place in life.
I will stand and be
a Proud Nobody!

ACKNOWLEDGMENTS

I would like to give a big shout-out to those behind the scenes who helped with this book. Yes, I wrote it, but many others helped bring it to reality: the editors, the proofreaders, the printers, the layout and cover designers, and the publisher. I'm sure there are others who have slipped my mind, but I want to recognize you all as somebodies. Thank you.

I would also like to give a huge thank-you to all the nobodies out there who play such an important part in our lives.

CPSIA information can be obtained
at www.ICGtesting.com
Printed in the USA
BVHW041023270322
632570BV00020B/298

9 781734 582970